HAL•LEONARD

Classical

PLAY-ALONG™

Volume 6

T0078945

Wolfgang Amadeus
MOZART
(1756-1791)

Horn Concerto in D Major, K 412/514

ISBN 978-1-4234-6242-2

HAL•LEONARD®
CORPORATION

7777 W. BLUEMOUND RD. P.O. BOX 13819 MILWAUKEE, WI 53213

In Australia Contact:
Hal Leonard Australia Pty. Ltd.
4 Lentara Court
Cheltenham, Victoria, 3192 Australia
Email: ausadmin@halleonard.com.au

For all works contained herein:
Unauthorized copying, arranging, adapting, recording or public performance is an infringement of copyright.
Infringers are liable under the law.

Visit Hal Leonard Online at
www.halleonard.com

Preface

The Hal Leonard Classical Play-Along™ series allows you to work through great classical works systematically and at any tempo with accompaniment.

Tracks 2-3 on the CD demonstrate the concert version of each movement. After tuning your instrument to Track 1 you can begin practicing the piece. Using the Amazing Slow-Downer technology included on the CD, you can adjust the recording to any tempo you like without altering the pitch. (Note that when using Amazing Slow-Downer, the CD will stop after each track instead of playing continuously.)

- Track No. ☐1 – tuning notes
- Track numbers in circles ◯ – concert version
- Track numbers in diamonds ◆ – play-along version

CONCERT VERSION

Gleb Karpushkin, Horn

Russian Philharmonic Orchestra Moscow

Konstantin Krimets, Conductor

CONCERTO

for Horn in D Major, KV 412 / 514 (386b)

I ②

W.A. Mozart (1756-1791)

© 2000 by DOWANI, Liechtenstein

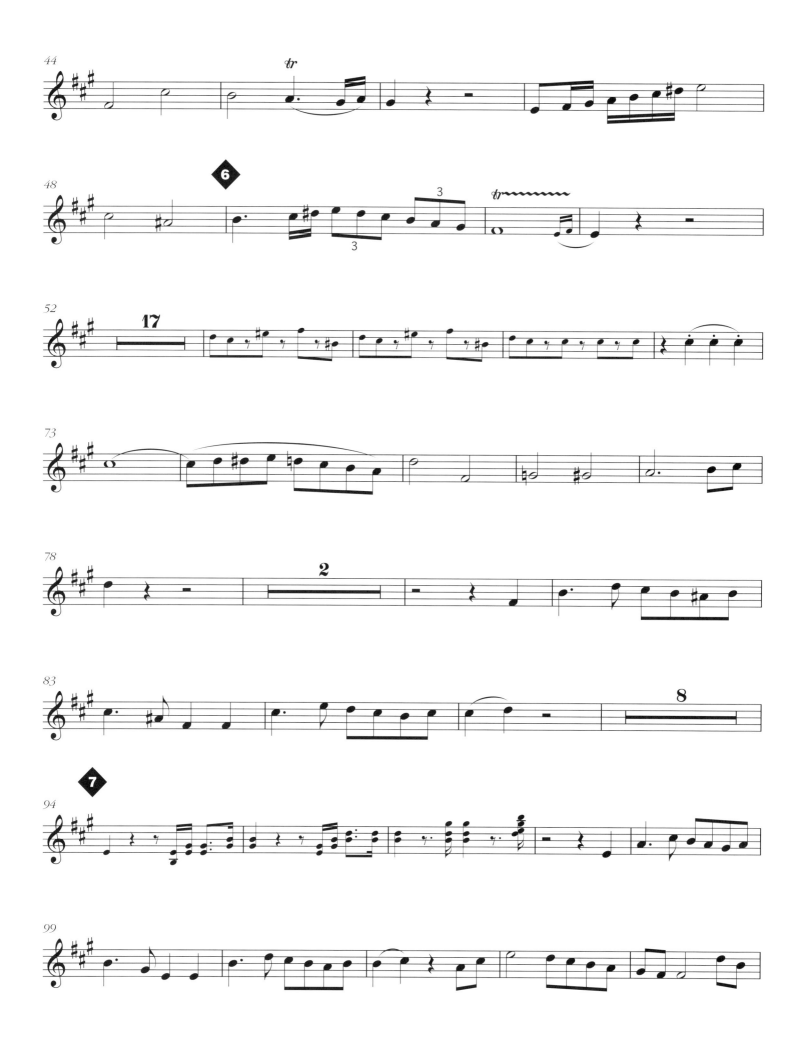